Testimonia

GW00656550

Understandin₍

(*A Guide for Male Survival*)

"Finally, assembled in one place are all of the mysteries of womanhood that men have failed to understand since the beginning of time. And the authors insure that they still remain mysteries. The odd man who isn't secure in his cluelessness will take heart in the knowledge that he isn't alone, he isn't even odd - he's just like every man who's ever drawn a breath."

~ Pete Morin, author of ***Diary of a Small Fish*** and other stories.

"Having immersed myself in the wit and wisdom of Understanding Women, I can work out where I've gone wrong in life. Now I know that if men are from Mars, women are from wherever in the hell they decide to be at any given moment. A man can't win — but he can learn how to go with the flow if he gets on board with this survival manual".

~ Andy Lake, author of ***Shades of Green***.

"My mind cramped with knowledge after reading this. Now my wife wants to talk more ... a big sarcastic thanks to all involved in this book!"

~ E.J. Findorff, Author of **Unhinged**

Understanding Women

~

(A Guide for Male Survival)

This literary piece of work, which is based on the combined author's creative intellect, should not be taken solely as gospel, as no two relationships are identical. In addition, as no names, places, characters or incidents were mentioned herein, no disclaimers are hereby warranted.

Any resemblance to actual relationships was fully intended. This was necessary so that we could propagate our intended findings, which are intended to assist the male species' quest for survival and harmonious relationships with females.

ISBN—Paperback: 978-0-9855412-2-4 (13 digit)
            : 0985541229 (10 digit)

Library of Congress Control Number: 2013914084

Printed in the United States of America

This book is dedicated to all the males out there who haven't a clue when it comes to understanding the inner workings of women. And let's face it—that probably includes all males.

~ Foreword ~

How to better understand a Woman? Is it possible to get anywhere near a proper understanding? Perplexing questions that have gone unanswered since the time of Adam, The First. Well, not so perplexing that we couldn't find the answers through the course of our exhaustive and exhausting studies. And we are now prepared to share the fruits of our research with you.

History and scripture tell us that this problem has been around for ions. Eve ate of the juicy bits of the apple, all the soft stuff, and left Adam to eat the hardcore. As we know, all the tasty, tempting stuff is in the "flesh," and all the scientific, factual stuff is concentrated mainly in the CORE, which isn't meant here to mean the Congress of Racial Equality. This meant that the male species was left with only understanding simple facts, like engineering stuff, while women were left with all the touchy-feely, sweet stuff. We have since come to learn that this is a sexist, old-fashioned view, and that it is absolutely disgusting to think that women are anything other than exactly racially equal. This modern view, however, doesn't really fit with this book, based on our uncovered facts, so we will ignore it. This book is, therefore, a historical-hysteric with scientific burps, rather than a proper, modern academic work.

So, if you care to join us, let us first take a glance back at the "fruitful" beginnings of men and women and where the problems actually began.

At this point, we must consider what would have happened if neither of them had learnt how "beneficial" it is to eat apples. If the first man and woman hadn't become sexual-elated, then none of us would be here today. Everything must have seemed sort of logical to Adam and Eve—not that anyone really knew much about logic before the Greeks. In fact, in those days, before feelings and science got all mixed up, everything must have seemed perfectly straightforward. Gardening is a very bio and logical experience and, before sex, tennis and Monopoly, there wouldn't have been much to do except gardening anyway.

They certainly lived the simple life before the forbidden fruit got munched. The tree of knowledge is perhaps best thought of as a sort of library, and the particular apple that Eve munched on was taken from the shelf labeled Sin. The first sign of things going wrong between the sexes was actually seen on that very same evening, as Adam lay in Eve's bed, loins at the ready, Eve probably rolled over and said, "Not tonight Adam, I have a headache."

For millions of years the male species has paid the price for the transgressions of one woman, Eve. And as all men know, things have never gotten any easier. So that is why, following years of painstaking research, we offer you this condensed version of **Understanding Women (A Guide for Male Survival)**. Why a condensed version you ask? That is easily answered. Well-researched studies have conclusively found that the male species has an attention span maxing out at around 60 seconds--unless watching sports with beer and snacks in hand. If any reader would like to read the longer version of this book, running to 1489 small print pages, just send us a note with your check for $682.32. Postage and handling are generously included.

Unlike other "motivational" or "self-help" books that generally don't get read (being too long and boring), this book will keep you transfixed from beginning to end. Every single chapter will answer in explicit, easy to understand detail, the answers to "understanding women" that have been missed by all males since the dawn of Man "One." No longer will you enter into a relationship blindly—as you will have the answers right from the start. Warning: It may result in your thinking twice about even entering into a relationship. Failure to read these pages, in their entirety, could result in a life of pain and acute mental suffering – for which we the authors cannot be held liable.

The following 101 statements, as you will quickly note, contains what we believe are the most perplexing questions asked by 96.384% of all males. Multiple research studies have proven conclusively that the questions and answers contained within, cover all nationalities, all religions, all races, and all shapes and styles of sexual fittings. If you are a breathing male anywhere in this universe – these questions and corresponding answers will apply to YOU. Our goal in writing this book, first and foremost, was to assist you in achieving the highest forms of understanding in your respective relationships. Should you choose to ignore the advice contained within these pages – you do so at your own peril. If you are known to have masochistic tendencies, then read no further. Our desire is not to deny you the self-inflicted anguish and pains that apparently bring you great pleasure.

In conclusion, *Understanding Women (A Guide for Male Survival)* should clearly undo the ravages inflicted on the male species by Eve. If for any reason you are not helped by the advice given within, then we can only conclude that you are just too much of a man's man. This book is only meant to help men who prefer to stay on top, and who have the missionary steel to learn to do things better.

We strongly encourage you to buy a second copy for your best mate, you know, the one that just got separated from his soul mate, cell-mate, playmate, his consum-mate, or whatever.

Sincerely (& Best Wishes),

Michael R. Jennings, Jody E. Lebel & Richard Bunning

#1

What's left of your brain when you begin to believe that she really will be ready in five minutes?

Answer

Mush. Everyone knows that a woman's five minutes is equal to a quarter in a football game.

#2

What gift for a woman will get you in the dog house the fastest?

Answer

A weight-loss video.

#3

What should you say when a women is in a bitchy mood?

Answer

The few survivors suggest the answer is, "nothing." And, if possible, vacate the area immediately.

#4

In a woman's mind, what does a man think about besides sex?

Answer

This is a trick question. Men think about sex all the time ... and everyone knows that.

#5

What to expect from a woman when you forget your anniversary.

Answer

364 days of reminders.

#6

How will you know when the honeymoon
is long over?

Answer

You kind of hope she leaves the nightgown
on.

#7

Why do men struggle to understand feminism?

Answer

It's really no struggle at all. Men just don't understand it. And most likely never will.

#8

What does your woman mean when she ends a "discussion" with the word "fine?"

Answer

In short, it means you're screwed -- and not in a nice way.

#9

Your woman asks you to fix something.
How do you know how long it will take you
to complete the requested task?

Answer

The answer will depend on how many rolls of duct tape you have in the junk drawer.

#10

Do you know how to write either a love letter or poem?

Answer

We thought so.

#11

What men understand about buying gifts for women?

Answer

Absolutely nothing—unless it is for himself or a buddy. The only thing he knows for sure is that his wallet is going to hurt.

#12

Why are women so apprehensive about receiving gifts from men?

Answer

They don't particularly like fishing poles and beer-brewing kits.

#13

Why men aren't praised for putting the toilet seat down.

Answer

Because she only notices when it's up. So remember that (which you probably won't).

#14

What men know about saying sorry?

Answer

Sorry is a word not likely to be found in the male dictionary. The "wronger" a man knows he is, the less likely he is to say he's sorry.

#15

When a woman is really angry with you, why does just saying you're sorry not always work?

Answer

Even using your best 'puppy eyes' won't cut it because a bouquet of flowers is required—or good jewelry if you're really in trouble. All of which will take a serious bite out of your beer-drinking money. Advice: Don't get her angry.

#16

What women mean by, "We'll talk about it later."

Answer

When ready, she will talk and you will listen.

#17

What a man gets when he's caught looking at a beautiful woman.

Answer

Having just entered dangerous territory, you can now expect no nookie for at least a week.

#18

Someone called her about your being seen chatting up a girl when you were out with the boys last night. What do you say when she confronts you about this "girl?"

Answer

She's not going to believe anything you
have to say, but you can try this line anyway: "That girl was working her way
through college. I just wanted to help her
out; and besides, John made me do it."

#19

Why do women not believe men when they say they just went to the strip club to relax?

Answer

No one really believes that. Hell, you don't even believe that.

#20

What is going through her mind when you tell her she looks like Jennifer Lopez?

Answer

Deep down she knows you are just hoping to get lucky.

#21

What does a woman believe when a man tells her she's the only one he thinks of when they're in bed?

Answer

He's lying, but if she's ready for a bit of action she rolls with it. Besides, it's just as well that he can't read her mind.

#22

Will she continue to satisfy your wildest fantasies as the years move along?

Answer

She doesn't now, so why would that change?

#23

When he says, "I will always fancy only you, honey," what is she thinking?

Answer

That he wants her to make a sandwich and bring him a cold beer.

#24

Will she open up if you ask her about her past love life?

Answer

Only if you use a crow bar or get her intoxicated. Even then it probably won't be truthful.

#25

The most likely consequence if you were dumb enough to ask her weight?

Answer

Not printable. If you dare to ask, you will soon be living the single life.

#26

Her answer when asked, "How much did you spend today, dear?"

Answer

I saved just enough to pay for your leisure activities for a week.

#27

What she really means when she says, "Behave in front of my girlfriends."

Answer

Be deeply UNinterested in their physical attractiveness or — you ... are ... dead ... meat.

#28

What happens when you say, "I had a hard week at work, so can I opt out of some chores?"

Answer

She doesn't understand the question. Best get busy.

#29

How to respond when she says, "Do I look fat in this?"

Answer

With a very fast and decisive NO. You should know the response by now. How old are you, anyway?

#30

What to expect in bed after you get back from a late night hockey game.

Answer

More frosty atmosphere and an icy bed.

#31

What can you expect after taking her out for a special occasion to a fast food place?

Answer

A slow burn for the rest of the evening.

#32

What to expect from a woman after your night out with your drunken (have a good-time) buddies.

Answer

At first, loud silence. But in the morning?
More loud, less silence.

#33

What should a man say when that "once a month" week comes around?

Answer

This is one we all learn the hard way. So the answer is "nothing." Just keep handing her the chocolates and keep quiet.

#34

What you can expect a woman to say when you yell for her to bring another beer.

Answer

Nothing.   But listen for the slam of a door.

#35

What response will you get when talking sports, cars and Playboy centerfolds?

Answer

Hard to answer as she will be intentionally out of earshot. Or you will see rolled eyes and hear loud zzzzzzzz sounds.

#36

What she will think when she views your body ten years into the relationship?

Answer

"And he wants ME to lose a few pounds?"

#37

What goes through a woman's mind after the honeymoon is over?

Answer

Those thongs are headed for the trash can.

#38

What men know about sustaining a romantic relationship?

Answer

Um . . . What exactly does romantic mean?
Beer causes romance, doesn't it?

#39

Why is it that men can never find the G-spot?

Answer

Because it is unnecessarily far off the most straightforward route map.

#40

What happens when you tell a woman that she is lucky to have you in her life?

Answer

That is difficult to answer as so many expressions can look like utter disbelief.

#41

What to expect sexually when your woman catches you viewing porn on your computer.

Answer

You'll be having sex with yourself.

#42

Because you feel that you are smarter than the average bear, you almost always know exactly what your woman is saying, right?

Answer

Just who are you trying to kid, buddy? You
will never know what a woman is really trying to say—even they don't. Advice: Keep
your thoughts to yourself at all costs.

#43

What is it, specifically, that men don't understand about women?

Answer

Everything about "women."

#44

Do you believe the concept that Men are from Mars and Women are from Venus?

Answer

Probably not, because you have no idea where those places are.

#45

When is the best time to ask her if she has had a busy day?

Answer

Right after you clean out the garage and mow the lawn.

#46

Should you ever tell your woman that she reminds you of her mother?

Answer

Any comparison is dangerous, but that one is a minefield. Go walk the dog or something, find some space until you come to your senses, you idiot.

#47

On which special occasion should you buy your woman a useful kitchen appliance as a gift?

Answer

On the occasion of you moving out. You are allowed to collect all your stuff off the front lawn.

#48

When is it appropriate to compare your woman's cooking to your mother's?

Answer

Only if the other woman isn't around. Naturally, only say anything if the one you are with does the recipe best.

#49

Men are motivated when they feel needed, while women are motivated when they feel cherished. How does the average guy deal with this?

Answer

Kill two birds with one stone. Slay some spiders.

#50

Do you know how to act like a white knight?

Answer

Yes, killing spiders helps, but going out and buying her that emergency supply of tampons is the real answer.

#51

Is it true that wedding plans generally take care of themselves?

Answer

If you answered yes, take heart, it's not the end of the world being a life-long bachelor.

52

Do you know how to find a good jewelry store as opposed to a mall kiosk?

Answer

Let's put it this way—would you buy your golf clubs from Toys-R-Us?

#53

Why do women like it when you hold their hand at the mall?

Answer

To stop you from wandering off to the bar.

#54

Why does she get angry when you pull over to the side of the road to take a leak?

Answer

The world is not your urinal. She doesn't want people to see what a moron she's with. Besides, she has to plan for her calls of nature, dumbo. So why shouldn't you?

#55

Why is it that men can't find things and women know exactly where they are?

Answer

It's hard for a man to tell the difference between a laundry basket and the floor.

Why do women love shoes and handbags?

Answer

No one can really answer this one. Just accept it. And when she asks you which pair of shoes matches her outfit better —for gawd's sake, just pick one. Whatever you pick, she'll go with the other one anyway.

Where do empty milk cartons live?

Answer

No—not in the fridge, apparently.

#58

Let's try another one. How do ice cubes get in those tiny square trays?

Answer

Of course you know how, it's the "who does the how" that is confusing.

59

Why do women cry at the drop of a hat?

Answer

This is really difficult for most men to understand; because even if a man gets his arm caught in a wood chipper, he's not allowed to cry.

#60

What do you do when your woman is crying and you can't figure out the reason?

Answer

Comfort cuddle. You don't know what this is, do you?   Okay, second choice; take out your wallet, pull out a credit card and call out for dinner.

#61

Why do most men hate to dance?

Answer

They don't if it leads to horizontal dancing later; if there is an end goal then dancing becomes a sport.

#62

What is so hard about calling your woman if you're going to be coming home late?

Answer

It's difficult to dial with a beer in one hand, a lap dancer on your lap, and all the noise of the buddies egging you on.

#63

Your woman tells you she has just read a new study that found that men who share in the housework are happier. What is your reaction?

Answer

Tell her you believe that dust is a harmless, natural occurrence and you're an all natural kind of man.

#64

Why do women want you to watch senti-
mental movies with them?

Answer

They're hoping you will take notes and be more romantic at home. There's nothing funny about that answer. It's just the truth, but unlikely to have any real effect on you.

#65

What is water retention?

Answer

Hint: it's not when the ice melts and waters down your drink. You actually don't know, do you?

#66

Why do women not trust their men to wash clothes?

Answer

Most men have no idea there are different cycles in the washing machine and can't tell laundry detergent from dish soap.

67

Why do women hate it when you hog the TV remote?

Answer

They would love to be caressed by you the way you do that damn remote.

#68

Why do most men hate cats?

Answer

Cats spend all day sleeping on the couch. Men want to spend all day sleeping on the couch.

#69

Why does she not like your dog?

Answer

You rub the dog's belly more than hers.

#70

How can you tell if she's faking her orgasm?

Answer

The answer is you can't. To make up for it men fake their finances.

#71

What should a man never say to a woman in the gym?

Answer

"If you really want to get your heart rate up, I've got something for you." Note to the Gym Rats out there: The only thing coming up will be her lunch.

#72

What should a man never say to a waitress?

Answer

"I'll take a jumbo burger, an order of cheese fries, and a side of you." You can bet ten to one that she will spit in your food ... or worse.

#73

When is it okay to ask a woman, "Are those real?"

Answer

Only when talking about another woman's diamonds.

Two things you should never say to a tall woman.

Answer

Well at least you're not overly wide. What's
the weather like up there?

When your woman is in an unlovable mood, do you still put your arm around her and pull her close?

Answer

It's worth a try if there's the slightest chance for a bit of action.

#76

Why does TV channel surfing drive your woman crazy?

Answer

Unless they are hilarious or have nearly naked women in them, men hate to watch commercials. With all the clicking around, your woman is sure to miss some important part in her show, and that means your night is going to go south.

#77

When you come home late and are totally blitzed, and she's in the doorway with crossed arms and one eyebrow raised, what do you do?

Answer

Blame it all on your buddies, or the medicine you're taking to improve your libido.

#78

Why doesn't she like your collection of t-shirts?

Answer

Because she doesn't want to be seen with a man who wears "It Takes a Real Man with Balls to Get a Vasectomy," "Lock Up Your Daughters," "I've Got Wood," "My Other Car's a Ferrari," "Harvard University," "Star Trekkie," or "Black Sabbath."

When should you stop getting tattoos?

Answer

When you have the complete cast of Looney Tunes characters on your butt.

Why will your woman try to change the way you dress yourself?

Answer

To show other women that she keeps a tidy house. And that includes the slob she is living with.

#81

Your woman lets out a little scream in the bathroom while running water for her bath. What is your best guess about what's going on in there?

Answer

She just noticed the tide line of engine oil you left. It's a good time to make a beer run.

#82

Why doesn't she like your best buddy/mate?

Answer

She doesn't want to hear stories about what an idiot you've been. He represents the world before she began adapting you to her will.

#83

What are the consequences of her going to bed mad following an argument?

Answer

Two choices actually: A night without lovemaking or a night on the couch.

#84

What is it about men and their cars that women don't understand?

Answer

Cars don't tell them what to do.

#85

When should you say you're sorry and when should you hold your ground?

Answer

Say you're sorry when there's no way out of your being wrong. Hold your ground when you know you're wrong but she can't prove it.

#86

Why does she like the thermostat setting on high?

Answer

Being around you creates a chill because you're not as hot as you think you are. Besides, you're only happy when she's not wearing her woolly tights.

87

Why do women always want to see a man's Facebook info?

Answer

To see if he erased his old contacts. No need to tell her about the cloud account, right?

#88

Should a man keep a separate bank account?

Answer

Yes, you may need the money for when she takes out the restraining order against you.

#89

Why are women so fussy about where things go?

Answer

For the same reason you can't find your socks, your keys or your checkbook. They're in a pile somewhere.

#90

Your probable answer to a woman's question, "Why don't you tell me you love me either before, during or after having sex?"

Answer

"Before ~ I'm too excited. During ~ I'm too busy. After ~ I'm too tired.

#91

In a recent survey, we asked over 1000 males if it is possible to "really" make a woman totally happy.

Answer

Survey Says:

1) Not in your lifetime.

2) Only if your name is Robert Redford, Leonardo DiCaprio or Brad Pitt. Hell, they can't even do it. And if they can't, you sure as hell can't.

3) Only if she's had a frontal lobotomy.

4) Yes, but only when you walk out the door.

5) It will be a cold day in hell when you are able to make a woman happy if you are in a committed relationship.

92

When picking out something to wear, how do we know if the colors clash?

Answer

A man doesn't have to be able to tell if colors clash. The woman will do it for him.

#93

What do you say when she asks you to guess her dress size?

Answer

In your head, consider what you really think that number is ...then deduct 4 sizes.

#94

How do you pretend that you are both understanding and listening to her every word?

Answer

Keep your eyes open and your mouth shut.
Just smile and nod every once in a while.

When should you offer to help your woman around the house?

Answer

Only if the game you're watching is already won/lost.

When shouldn't you offer to help your woman?

Answer

Any time you can avoid chores. Men have a shorter life span than women, so why waste your precious time volunteering when you could be out golfing?

#97

Your dog threw up on the carpet. What does your woman say while handing you a wad of paper towels?

Answer

I see he takes after his master.

#98

What do you do when you forget what it was she wanted you to pick up?

Answer

Either buy flowers or tell her you were ac-
costed by thugs but broke loose. Anything
but the truth.

#99

Who can she swear at, but you can't?

Answer

Her mother. And you had better remember that.

#100

Why does she want a house with a garden?

Answer

To keep you out from under her feet.

#101

Why do you think she will eventually pres-
sure you for a larger house?

Answer

Less chance of her running into you.

About the Authors

Michael R. Jennings. He was born and raised in Seattle, Washington. He received his Master's degree in Sociology from the University of Colorado in 1974. Michael is the author of a romance novel, *Flight Surgeon*, which was released in late 2011(available through Amazon and other sources). Following an 18 month stint in Scottsdale, he now resides in Great Falls, Virginia—just outside of D.C. — where he is now chief cook, housekeeper, maintenance man and dog walker for his two grown sons. What was he thinking?
Author Website: http://flightsurgeonnovel.com/

Jody E. Lebel. Following years as a travel agent, Jody Lebel returned to school and became a court reporter, swapping traveling to exotic locations for reporting the cases of murderers, rapists, and thieves. Being assigned to the chief judge in Broward County exposed her to a wide spectrum of humanity; from funny to tragic to bizarre to downright creepy. She has reported everything from a homeless guy who had jumped the turnstile on the Metrorail and was now in jail for not having a quarter, to the Tamiami Strangler, a serial killer who murdered six women. In court, the stories she is exposed to, the mayhem, the heartbreak, and particularly the black humor all make writing a breeze--and she almost never falls asleep at the keyboard anymore. On a personal note, Jody was raised in charming New England, was an only child who had an only child (claiming she didn't breed well in captivity) and now lives with her two cats in a high-rise alongside the ocean in southern Florida. Find her latest novel, *Playing Dead*, on Amazon.com.

Author Website: www.jodylebel.com or
http://wwmysterystory.blogspot.com/

Richard Bunning. Richard only started publishing stuff when well into his mid-life crisis; a crisis that seems set to run right up to the full-time whistle. By the time the "I got story" disease struck, he had cleared hurdles imposed by the study of International Relations, driving tractors, nutrition research, pig feeding, and being substituted on as full-time care for his kids. Their Mum brings in the now metaphorical bacon and still does the ironing.

Richard himself was mostly grown in the East of England, since then he has inflicted himself on the people of New Zealand and latterly Switzerland. Writing started as meddling with English versions of neoclassical French plays. Some of these revisions have been published. This endeavor grew out of nothing more academic than a naïve and unsuccessful attempt to help his children cope with the traumas of adapting to a French language education. Completely independently of each other, the kids and books blossomed. More recently, the real nature of this strange writer has emerged through speculative science fiction and short stories.

This is the first time that Richard has been in a cooperative venture with real professionals. He was fortunate indeed that Jennings and Lebel were prepared to take on a charity case.

Author Website:
http://richardbunningbooksandreviews.weebly.com

Printed in Great Britain
by Amazon